MONEY SKILLS FOR

KIDS

Chapter 1: Understanding Money: Where It Comes From and Why It's Important

Welcome to the fascinating world of money, young reader! This isn't just a book about coins and banknotes; it's about understanding what money really is, where it comes from, and why it's so crucial in our lives. Money isn't just for adults; the earlier you learn about it, the better you can use it when you grow up. Ready to dive in? Let's get started!

What is Money?

You may think money is just those shiny coins and colorful notes that adults use to buy things, but there's a lot more to it. Money is a system of trade, and it helps us exchange goods and services. Imagine if we didn't have money, and you wanted to trade your comic books for a new skateboard. It would be tough to find someone who has a skateboard and wants your exact comic books, right? That's why we use money. You sell your comic books to someone who wants them, get money for it, and then use that money to buy a skateboard. Simple and efficient!

The History of Money

Believe it or not, there was a time when money didn't exist! People used to barter, which means they traded things they had for things they needed. If you were a farmer who grew apples, and you needed shoes, you would have to find a shoemaker who needed apples. As you can guess, this was quite inconvenient!

Over time, people started using items like gold, silver, or even seashells as a medium of exchange because they were rare and people valued them. This was the beginning of what we now call "money".

As societies grew and evolved, so did money. People started using coins, then paper money, and now most money is digital - numbers on a computer screen!

Why is Money Important?

Money is essential for several reasons. It allows us to buy goods and services, helps us save for the future, and makes trading easier. Money also gives us a way to compare the value of different things. For example, a bicycle is worth more than a candy bar. But how much more? Money gives us a way to measure this.

Furthermore, money is a crucial part of how a country's economy works. Governments use money to provide services to their people, businesses use money to buy resources and pay their employees, and individuals like your parents use money to buy food, clothes, and other things the family needs.

Now that we have covered the basics of what money is and why it's important, in the next chapter, we will learn about different types of money and how they work. We'll discuss cash, bank accounts, and even digital currencies like Bitcoin! We are on an exciting journey to understanding the world of money, and there is so much more to learn. Let's keep going!

Chapter 2: The Importance of Saving: Your Money's Safe House

In the previous chapter, we learned about what money is, where it comes from, and why it's important. It was a fun journey, wasn't it? Now let's dive deeper into the world of money. This chapter is all about saving. You might have heard adults in your life talk about savings, or you may have seen a piggy bank and wondered why we put coins in there. Let's get all those questions answered!

What is Saving?

Imagine you really want to buy a new video game or a toy, but it costs more money than you have right now. What do you do? You could wait until your birthday or a holiday and hope someone gives it to you as a gift. Or you could save money over time and buy it yourself!

Saving money means setting aside a part of the money you receive, like your allowance or birthday money, instead of spending it all right away. You keep adding to your savings over time, little by little, until you have enough for what you want or need.

Why Should You Save?

Why can't we just spend the money we have? Here are some reasons why saving is important:

1. **To Buy Something Expensive:** Sometimes, there are things we want that cost more than the money we have right now, like a new bicycle or a video game console. By saving a little bit of money regularly, we can reach our goal and buy what we want.

2. **For Unexpected Events:** Life can surprise us. Maybe your soccer ball gets punctured, and you need to buy a new one. Or perhaps you lose a

school book and need to replace it. Having savings can help us during such unexpected events.

3. For The Future: As we grow older, our needs and wants grow too. Perhaps you'll want to buy a car when you're older or go to college. Starting to save from a young age can help you prepare for those future needs.

Where Can You Save Money?

Now that we know why we should save, let's talk about where we can save our money.

1. **Piggy Banks:** A piggy bank is a classic place to start saving. It's a fun way to see your money grow as the piggy bank gets heavier with the coins and notes you put in.

2. **Savings Account:** As you grow older and your savings increase, your parents or guardians can help you open a savings account in a bank. This is a safe place to keep your money. Plus, the bank pays you a little extra money called "interest" for keeping your money with them.

3. **Jars or Envelopes:** You can also save by using different jars or envelopes for different goals. For example, you might have one jar for a new skateboard, another for a video game, and so on.

Tips to Help You Save

1. Start Small: You don't need a lot of money to start saving. Even a small amount, saved regularly, can add up over time.

2. Set Goals: It's easier to save when you know what you're saving for. Set clear goals, like buying a new toy, donating to a cause you care about, or even starting your college fund.

3. Be Patient: Saving takes time, and that's okay! It's exciting to see your money grow as you get closer to your goal.

Remember, money is a tool, and saving is a skill that helps you use this tool wisely. In the next chapter, we'll learn about budgeting, which is another essential money skill. Until then, happy saving!

Chapter 3: The Art of Budgeting: Planning Your Money

Hello there, young savers! In our last chapter, we explored the world of saving money and why it's essential. But just saving isn't enough, we also need to plan how we use our money. This is where budgeting comes in. Let's find out what budgeting is and why it's an important skill to have!

What is Budgeting?

Have you ever planned to do something fun, like going on a trip or organizing a party, and you had to decide what things you needed and how much they would cost? That's essentially what budgeting is.

A budget is a plan that helps us decide how to spend our money. It involves dividing our money into different categories like saving, spending, and donating, according to what we think is most important. It's like a map that guides us in making money decisions.

Why is Budgeting Important?

Budgeting is important for several reasons:

1. It Helps You Reach Your Goals: If you're saving for something specific, like a new toy or a bicycle, budgeting helps you plan how much money you need to save and how long it will take to reach your goal.

2. It Prevents Overspending: By having a plan, you can make sure you don't spend too much on one thing and not have enough left for something else that's important to you.

3. It Gives You Control: Budgeting makes you the boss of your money! You get to decide where your money goes and what it does.

How to Make a Budget

Making a budget might sound like a grown-up thing to do, but it's actually pretty simple, and you can do it too! Here's how:

1. Identify Your Income: The first step in making a budget is to figure out how much money you have. This could be from your allowance, money gifts, or money you earn.

2. List Your Expenses: Next, make a list of the things you want to spend money on. This could be anything from buying toys, books, candy, or even saving for a future goal. Don't forget to include giving or donating if that's something you want to do.

3. Divide Your Money: Now, decide how much of your money will go into each category. You could use percentages, like 50% for saving, 30% for spending, and 20% for giving. Or you could decide specific amounts, like $2 for saving, $1 for spending, and $1 for giving.

4. Track Your Spending: Keep track of where your money is going. You can do this in a notebook or a jar with different compartments for each category.

Remember, a budget isn't a strict rule that you can't change. It's a plan that can be adjusted as you go along. Maybe you decide you want to save more for a bigger goal, or you want to spend a little extra on a special treat - that's okay! As long as you're thinking about it and making conscious decisions, you're budgeting.

In the next chapter, we'll learn about the difference between needs and wants when we spend our money. But for now, happy budgeting!

Chapter 4: Understanding Expenses: Needs Vs. Wants

Hi again, young savers! Now that we've learned about saving and budgeting, let's dive into another important money concept: understanding expenses. In this chapter, we'll learn about the difference between needs and wants. Let's get started!

What Are Expenses?

First things first, what are expenses? Expenses are the things we spend our money on. This could be something as simple as a candy bar or as important as a warm jacket for winter. All these things that we buy or spend money on are considered our expenses.

Needs Vs. Wants

Now, all expenses are not created equal. They can be divided into two categories: Needs and Wants.

Needs are things that are necessary for our survival and well-being. These are things we can't live without. Some examples are:

1. **Food and Water:** We need to eat and drink to stay alive and healthy.

2. **Shelter:** A place to live, like your home, is a need because it protects us from the weather and gives us a place to rest and grow.

3. **Clothing:** Clothes protect us from the weather and keep us comfortable.

4. **Health Care:** This includes any medicines or doctor visits needed to keep us healthy.

On the other hand, **Wants** are things that we would like to have but don't need for survival. These are things that often make life more enjoyable or comfortable. Some examples are:

1. **Toys and Video Games:** These are fun to have, but we can survive without them.

2. **Candy or Extra Snacks:** We might want these, but they aren't necessary for our health, especially if we're eating balanced meals.

3. **Designer Clothes:** While we need clothes, we don't necessarily need designer or brand-name ones.

4. Extravagant Holidays: While holidays are fun, they can be enjoyed in simple, inexpensive ways too.

Why is the Difference Important?

Understanding the difference between needs and wants is important because it helps us make better decisions about our spending. It's okay to spend money on wants, but it's crucial to make sure our needs are met first.

If we spend all our money on wants, we might not have enough left to cover our needs. This can lead to problems. For instance, spending all our money on toys and not having enough to buy a needed school book wouldn't be a smart choice.

Applying It to Your Budget

Remember the budget we talked about in the last chapter? Understanding needs and wants can help us plan our budget better. We can ensure we have enough money to cover our needs and then decide how to spend the rest on our wants.

In the next chapter, we'll talk about how you can make your money grow by investing it. But for now, try to think about your own needs and wants. Can you identify which of your expenses are needs and which are wants?

Chapter 5: The Power of Investing: Making Your Money Grow

Hey, future millionaires! We've already covered how money works, the importance of saving, how to budget, and the difference between needs and wants. Now, are you ready to learn about something super cool? Let's talk about making your money grow through investing!

What is Investing?

Imagine you plant a seed in a pot and water it every day. Over time, that seed grows into a plant. Now, if that plant is a fruit-bearing plant, one day, you'll get to enjoy delicious fruits from it.

Investing is a bit like planting that seed. When you invest, you're putting your money (the seed) into something (the pot) that you think will grow over time. Just like watering the plant, you might add more money to your investment over time. And, if all goes well, your investment will grow, just like the plant, and give you more money (the fruits) in the future.

How Does Investing Work?

Investing works by putting your money into things (called assets) that can increase in value over time. These assets can be various things like a business, real estate (houses or land), or the stock market (buying a small part of a company).

When you invest in these things, you're hoping that they will be worth more in the future than they are today. This increase in value is called a "return," and it's how your money grows through investing.

Why Should You Invest?

Now you might be thinking, "I'm just a kid, why should I worry about investing?" Well, even though you're young, it's never too early to learn about investing. Here's why:

1. **Grow Your Savings:** Investing can help your savings grow faster. If you put your savings in a piggy bank or under your mattress, it won't grow. But if you invest it, it can grow over time.

2. **Beat Inflation:** Inflation is when things get more expensive over time. If your money is just sitting and not growing, it might lose value

because of inflation. But, if you invest it and it grows, it can keep up with or even beat inflation.

3. Reach Your Goals Faster: If you're saving for a big goal, like buying a cool gadget, investing could help you reach that goal faster.

Are There Risks?

Just like your plant might not grow if you don't take care of it properly, investments can also go down in value. This is called investment risk. But don't worry, there are ways to manage this risk, and we'll learn about them as you grow older.

For now, the most important thing is to understand what investing is and why it can be a powerful tool for making your money grow. As you get older and start earning money, you can start thinking about making your first investments!

Remember, investing is a long-term game. It's not about getting rich quickly but about growing your wealth steadily over time. In the next chapter, we'll learn about another way to grow your wealth: earning money!

Chapter 6: Earning Money: Hard Work Pays Off!

Hello, young earners! Have you ever heard the saying, "Money doesn't grow on trees?" Well, it's true! Money has to be earned, and it usually involves some form of work. But hey, don't worry! Work can be fun, especially when you get to see the results of your hard work. Let's dive into the exciting world of earning money!

Why Earning Money is Important

Before we talk about how you can earn money, let's first understand why earning money is important:

1. Independence: Earning your own money gives you a sense of independence. You don't always have to ask your parents for money if you want to buy something.

2. Responsibility: Earning money teaches you to be responsible. You start to understand the value of money and how hard it can be to earn it.

3. Achievement: Earning your own money gives you a sense of achievement. It's a great feeling when you can buy something with the money you earned!

Ways Kids Can Earn Money

Now, let's discuss some ways that you, as a kid, can earn money. Always remember to ask your parents for permission before starting any of these money-making ventures.

1. Do Extra Chores: One of the easiest ways to earn money is by doing extra chores around the house. Maybe there are things that your parents would be willing to pay you to do, like washing the car or mowing the lawn.

2. Sell Crafts or Homemade Goods: If you're good at making things, why not sell them? This could be anything from homemade lemonade to handcrafted bracelets.

3. Recycling: Some recycling centers pay for items like cans and bottles. Not only can you earn money, but you're also helping the environment!

4. Help Neighbors: Many people are willing to pay for help with their chores. This could be anything from walking dogs to helping with gardening.

5. Save Birthday and Holiday Money: Instead of spending all your birthday or holiday money, save some of it. It's a simple and effortless way to increase your funds.

Remember, the goal isn't to make lots of money quickly. It's about understanding how work translates into earnings and the satisfaction that comes with it.

The Reward of Hard Work

When you earn money from your hard work, it feels rewarding. You start appreciating the things you buy with it even more because you know the effort that went into earning that money. Plus, you'll also learn valuable lessons about the importance of hard work and dedication.

Working hard doesn't just pay off in terms of money. It helps you develop skills, build character, and gain experiences that will be valuable in your life ahead.

Now that you know the joy and benefits of earning money, in our next chapter, we'll explore the beauty of sharing and donating some of your wealth!

Chapter 7: Giving and Donating: Sharing Your Wealth

Hey, young philanthropists! Now that you're becoming experts in managing money, let's talk about another important aspect of finance: giving and donating. This might seem a bit strange - why would you want to give away the money you worked so hard to earn? Well, let's find out!

The Joy of Giving

Did you ever share your favorite toy with a friend? Or perhaps, gave a part of your snack to a classmate who forgot theirs? Remember how happy it made them feel? And remember the warm, fuzzy feeling it gave you? That's the joy of giving!

Giving is not just about making others happy. It makes us feel good about ourselves. It teaches us to be compassionate, understanding, and kind. When we share our wealth with those who need it more, we contribute to making the world a better place. Isn't that an amazing thing?

The Difference Between Giving and Donating

You might be wondering, "Isn't giving and donating the same thing?" Well, they're similar, but there's a slight difference:

1. **Giving:** This usually involves sharing with people you personally know. It could be giving

your old toys to your younger sibling or sharing your birthday money with your best friend who wants to buy the latest video game.

2. Donating: This means giving to a cause or an organization. This could be a charity that helps animals, an organization that plants trees, or a fund that helps kids go to school. The money you donate often helps many people and makes a big difference.

How Can Kids Donate?

Even though you're kids, there are plenty of ways you can donate! Here are a few ideas:

1. **Charity Boxes**: Some stores have charity boxes near the checkout counters where you can donate spare change. Every little bit helps!

2. **Fundraising Events**: Schools often host fundraising events like bake sales or car washes. You can participate and donate the money you earn.

3. **Donate Old Toys and Clothes**: Instead of throwing away your old toys and clothes, donate them to a charity that helps other kids.

4. **Online Donations**: With your parents' help, you can donate to various causes online.

Remember, it's not about how much you donate. It's the thought and intention behind it that counts.

The Gift of Giving

Giving and donating are not just about money. It's about sharing your kindness, compassion, and love with others. It's about understanding that everyone has a role in making the world a better place.

Remember, the value of money isn't just in spending it, but also in sharing it with others. In the next chapter, we will learn about smart shopping and getting value for your money.

Chapter 8: Smart Shopping: Getting Value for Your Money

Hello, young shoppers! Now that you're learning all about money, it's time to understand the art of smart shopping. It's not just about spending money but making sure you get good value for it.

What is Smart Shopping?

Smart shopping means buying things wisely. It's about making sure you get the most value for the money you spend. It means you're thinking about your purchases, making good choices, and saving money where you can. Cool, right?

Why is Smart Shopping Important?

Smart shopping is important because:

1. It Saves Money: By making wise choices, you can save a lot of money. And you already know how important saving is!

2. It Teaches You to Make Good Decisions: When you shop smart, you learn to make decisions based on what you need and what gives you the best value, rather than just what you want.

3. It Helps You Avoid Waste: By buying only what you need, you avoid wasting both products and money.

How Can Kids Shop Smart?

Even as kids, there are ways you can practice smart shopping. Here are some tips:

1. **Compare Prices**: If you're buying a toy or a book, check prices at different stores or online. You might find the same thing at a lower price somewhere else!

2. **Think Before You Buy**: Ask yourself, "Do I really need this?" Sometimes, you might want to buy something just because it's new or your friends have it. But if you already have similar things at home, it might be better to save your money for something else.

3. **Look for Sales and Discounts**: Sometimes, stores have sales where you can buy things for less money. Keep an eye out for these!

4. Buy Quality, Not Just Cheap: Buying the cheapest thing isn't always the best. It's better to buy something a little more expensive that will last longer than to buy something cheap that will break quickly.

Practice Smart Shopping

Next time you go shopping with your parents or get some money to spend, try to use these smart shopping tips. You'll be surprised at how much money you can save!

And always remember, the real value of money is not just in spending it but in spending it wisely. In the next chapter, we will learn about the concept of credit, borrowing, and paying back money.

Chapter 9: The Concept of Credit: Borrowing and Paying Back Money

Hi, there, future finance whiz! Today, we're going to talk about a very important topic: credit. You might be thinking, "Credit? Isn't that a grown-up thing?" Yes, but it's never too early to start understanding these concepts. And don't worry, we're going to make it as easy and fun as possible!

What is Credit?

When we talk about credit, we're talking about borrowing money. Imagine your friend has a super cool new comic book that you really want to read, but you can't buy it right now. Your friend lets you borrow the comic, and you promise to return it next week. That's a bit like credit, but instead of a comic book, it's money!

When you use credit, a bank or another company lends you money to buy something now, and you promise to pay it back later, usually with a little extra. That extra is called interest.

Why Do People Use Credit?

People use credit for lots of reasons:

1. To buy expensive things: If someone wants to buy a house or a car, they might not have enough money saved up. So, they borrow the money (that's credit!) and pay it back over time.

2. For emergencies: Sometimes unexpected things happen, like a car breaking down or a pet getting sick. In these situations, credit can help cover the costs until they can pay it back.

3. To build a credit history: This is a record of how well you pay back money you borrow. When you're older, if you've shown that you can use credit responsibly and pay it back on time, it can help you when you need to borrow a larger amount of money.

The Importance of Paying Back

When you borrow money, it's very important to pay it back on time. If you don't, it can cause problems later. Just like if you borrowed your friend's comic book and didn't return it, they might not trust you to borrow anything again.

With money, it's the same thing. If you don't pay back money you borrowed, it can damage your credit history. This can make it harder for you to borrow money in the future.

A Little Credit Practice

Even as kids, you can practice understanding credit. No, we're not suggesting you borrow money! But you can play games where you "borrow" game money or items and pay them back later. You can also watch and learn as your parents handle credit, like using a credit card at a store.

Remember, credit can be a helpful tool, but it's important to use it wisely. In the next chapter, we're going to learn about protecting your money. Sounds like a superhero mission, right? It kind of is!

Chapter 10: Protecting Your Money: The Basics of Fraud Prevention

Hello there, future financial expert! We've learned so much about money already, and we're not done yet. Today, we're going to talk about something super important: protecting your money. This chapter might sound a little bit like a detective story, and that's because it sort of is!

What Does Protecting Your Money Mean?

When we talk about protecting your money, we're talking about keeping it safe from people who might want to take it without permission. These people are called fraudsters or scammers, and their tricks are called fraud or scams.

Different Types of Scams

There are many different ways that scammers try to take money from people. Here are a few examples:

1. Identity theft: This is when a scammer tries to pretend to be you so that they can take your money. They might try to get information like your name, address, or even your parent's credit card number.

2. Phishing: This is when a scammer pretends to be a trusted company, like a bank, to trick you into giving them your personal information.

3. Fake prizes: Scammers might tell you that you've won a prize, but ask for money or personal information before you can claim it. Remember, if something sounds too good to be true, it probably is!

How to Protect Your Money

Now that we know some of the tricks scammers use, let's talk about how we can protect our money:

1. Keep your information safe: Never share personal information like your address, phone number, or your parents' credit card number unless your parents say it's OK.

2. Ask questions: If you're not sure about something, ask an adult. It's better to be safe than sorry!

3. Be careful online: Just like in the real world, there can be scammers online, too. Always check with an adult before clicking on links or sharing information.

Practice Makes Perfect

Just like with the other things we've learned about money, practice can help you get better at protecting your money. You could play a game where you pretend to be a detective protecting your money from fraudsters, or even have a discussion with your parents about how they protect their money.

Remember, it's always better to be safe than sorry when it comes to protecting your money. In our next chapter, we're going to learn about planning for the future, so stay tuned!

Chapter 11: Planning for the Future: Why Retirement Savings Matter Even for Kids

Hello future finance genius! So far, we've learned about earning, saving, investing, and protecting our money. Today, we're going to take a big leap forward and talk about something you might think is a long, long way off – retirement. Yes, even kids can start thinking about retirement!

What is Retirement?

First off, let's understand what retirement is. It's a time in a person's life, usually when they get older, when they choose to stop working. During retirement, people rely on the money they've saved over their working years to cover their living expenses.

Why Should Kids Think About Retirement?

Now you might be asking, "I'm just a kid, why should I worry about retirement?" That's a fair question! Here's the thing, starting to save for retirement early gives your money more time to grow. Remember how we talked about the power of investing and how your money can multiply over time? That's exactly what we're aiming for with retirement savings!

How Can Kids Save for Retirement?

Alright, so how does a kid like you start saving for something as far-off as retirement? Here's a simple plan:

1. **Start a savings jar or bank:** Label it "Retirement Savings." Whenever you get money, whether it's from doing chores or as a gift, put a little into this jar.

2. Talk to your parents about a Custodial IRA: IRA stands for Individual Retirement Account. A Custodial IRA is a special type of account that adults can open for kids. The money in this account can grow over many years and be used when you're older and ready to retire.

3. Learn and practice good money habits: The habits you form now, like saving and budgeting, will help you all through your life. The sooner you start, the better you'll get at managing your money.

The Magic of Compound Interest

Remember compound interest from Chapter 5? It's like a superpower for your savings. If you start saving small amounts now, these amounts can become quite large by the time you're ready to retire. That's the magic of compound interest!

A Penny Saved is a Penny Earned

Remember this saying as you start your journey towards saving for your future. Every penny you save now is a step towards a comfortable and happy retirement.

Don't worry, it's okay to dream about the future while enjoying your present. As a kid, your main job is to learn and have fun. But while you're at it, why not also get a head start on securing your future?

Chapter 12: Bonus: Fun Money Games and Activities

Hello there, future finance whizzes! We've learned a lot about money, but learning doesn't always have to be serious – it can be fun too! Let's try some cool money games and activities that will make learning about money even more exciting. Ready? Let's jump in!

1. The Coin Sorting Game

All you need for this game are some coins and a few bowls. Mix up a handful of coins and then race against the clock to see how quickly you can sort them into the correct bowls. This game is great for learning to recognize different coin values.

2. The Budgeting Challenge

Next time you go shopping with your parents, ask them if you can help plan the shopping list. Try to stick to a budget and make choices about what to buy based on price and necessity. This is a practical way to learn about budgeting and expenses.

3. The Lemonade Stand

A classic! Set up a lemonade stand and practice earning money. You can learn about investing in ingredients, setting a price, advertising, and making a profit. Plus, it's a tasty way to make some money!

4. Play Store

Gather some of your toys and pretend they are items in a store. Use play money to "buy" and "sell" the items. This will help you understand the concept of price and value.

5. Money Bingo

Create a bingo sheet with various coins and bills in the boxes. Draw pictures of money from a bag, and whoever gets a line of money values first, wins!

6. The Saving Game

Set a savings goal and try to reach it! This could be something like buying a new book, toy, or saving for a fun outing. This is a real-world way to practice saving and patience.

Remember, the goal of these games and activities is not only to have fun but also to reinforce everything we've learned about money. So, while you're laughing and playing, remember the important lessons behind each game.

The best part is that as you grow older, you'll come up with even more fun ways to learn about and manage your money. The world of finance can be a playground if you approach it with the right attitude!

Chapter 13: Your Money Journey: Path to Financial Independence

Hey there, young money master! We've gone through a lot in our journey. We've learned about where money comes from, the importance of saving, how to budget and differentiate between needs and wants, the power of investing, how hard work pays off, the joy of sharing, smart shopping, understanding credit, how to protect our money, why it's never too early to think about retirement, and even some fun money games!

But remember, this book is just the start of your journey to financial independence. So, what's the next step? Well, let's find out!

Take Charge of Your Money

As you get older, you'll have more and more opportunities to manage your money. Maybe you'll get a weekly allowance or a part-time job. Whatever happens, remember the lessons from this book. Budget wisely, save regularly, understand your needs and wants, and spend smartly.

Never Stop Learning

The world of money can be complex, but don't let that scare you. You've already taken the first step by reading this book. Keep on learning about money. There are tons of resources out there – books, websites, podcasts, and videos. As you grow up, your understanding of money will grow too.

Make Goals and Plan for the Future

Remember our chapter about saving for retirement? That might seem a long way off now, but it's never too early to start planning. Make goals for your money, both short-term (like saving for a new toy or book) and long-term (like saving for college or even retirement!). It's amazing how much you can achieve when you start early.

Keep It Fun

Lastly, never forget that managing your money can be fun! Whether you're running a lemonade stand or playing money bingo, remember to enjoy the journey. The world of finance is like a game – and you're learning to be a champion.

You're on an exciting path, and the sky's the limit. Stay curious, ask questions, and keep learning.

Remember, you are the boss of your money, not the other way around. You're on your way to financial independence, and that's something to be excited about!

We're so proud of you for taking the first steps on this journey. Remember, every financial wizard started just like you, learning the basics and building from there. So keep going, stay excited, and enjoy the journey!